AUTHENTIC

Dream Interpretations

From the Works of Ibn al-Qayyim & Al-Baghawī

Explained by Shaykh 'Abdullāh ibn Jāru Allāh

AUTHENTIC

Dream Interpretations

From the Works of Ibn al-Qayyim & Al-Baghawī

Explained by Shaykh ʻAbdullāh ibn Jāru Allāh

ISBN: 978-1-7923-3365-1

First Edition: Rajab 1441 A.H. / March 2020 C.E.

Cover Design: Usul Design
E-mail: info@usuldesign.com

Translator: Rasheed Barbee

Editing & Formatting: Razan Gregory
razangregory.com

Publisher's Information:

Authentic Statements Publishing
P. O. Box 15536
Philadelphia, PA. 19131
215.382.3382
215.382.3782-Fax

Store:
5000 Locust Street (Side Entrance)
Philadelphia, Pa 19139

Website: www.authenticstatements.com
E-mail: info@authenticstatements.com

TRANSLITERATION TABLE

Consonants

ء	'	د	d	ض	ḍ	ك	k
ب	b	ذ	dh	ط	ṭ	ل	l
ت	t	ر	r	ظ	ẓ	م	m
ث	th	ز	z	ع	‘	ن	n
ج	j	س	s	غ	gh	ه	h
ح	ḥ	ش	sh	ف	f	و	w
خ	kh	ص	ṣ	ق	q	ي	y

Vowels

Short	ـَ	a	ـِ	i	ـُ	u
Long	ـَا	ā	ـِي	ī	ـُو	ū
Diphthongs	ـَي	ay	ـَو	aw		

Glyphs

ﷺ *Sallallāhu ‘alayhi wa sallam* (May Allāh’s praise & salutations be upon him)
عليه السلام *‘Alayhis-salām* (Peace be upon him)
عز وجل *‘Aza wa jal* (Mighty and Majestic)
رضي الله عنه *Radiyallāhu ‘anhu* (May Allāh be pleased with him)
رضي الله عنها *Radiyallāhu ‘anha* (May Allāh be pleased with her)
رحمه الله *Rahimahullah* (May Allāh have mercy upon him)

TABLE OF CONTENTS

Types of Dreams 9
Truthful Dreams 9
Seeing the Prophet ﷺ 11
Good and Hated Dreams 12
Falsifying Dreams 14
Narrating Good Dreams 15
Etiquettes for Good Dreams 22
Etiquettes for Nightmares 23
Six Things to Do After Having a Nightmare 24
Dreams Come to Pass According to How They Are Interpreted 25
Dream Interpretation Explained by Al-Baghawi 31
Dream Interpretation from the Qur'ān 31
Dream Interpretation from the Sunnah 35
Dream Interpretation from the Proverbs of the People 36
Dream Interpretation According to Names 38
Dream Interpretation According to Meaning 39
Dream Interpretation According to the Opposite 39

Dream Interpretation Changing Due to an Addition or Subtraction 41

Dream Interpretation According to the Condition of the Person Dreaming 42

Dream Interpretation Explained by Ibn al-Qayyim 45

Dream Interpretation of the Pious Predecessors 52

ABOUT THE AUTHOR

He is the noble Shaykh ‘Abdullāh ibn Jāru Allāh ibn 'Ibrāhīm 'Āli Jāru Allāh. His lineage connects to the tribe of an-Nawāsir from Banī Tamīn. He was born in the province of al-Midhnab, in the city of al-Qasīm, and was raised with a righteous upbringing. He began studying in elementary school, as a youth, and memorized the Qur'ān by way of his father.

He traveled to the city of Riyadh during the year 1949, according to the Gregorian calendar (1368 Hijri). In the year 1955, he began taking knowledge from Shaykh Muḥammad ibn 'Ibrāhīm 'Āli Shaykh; the Grand Mufti of Saudi Arabia from 1953 until his death in 1969. In the year 1956, he enrolled in the Imām of Dawah Institute, now known as Al-Imām Muḥammad bin Sa‘ūd Islāmic University. He studied under a number of scholars, including Shaykh Ismaīl ibn Muḥammad al-Anṣārī and others.

He graduated from the Institute in the year 1960 and then enrolled in the college of Shariah in Riyadh. After graduating in the year 1965, he was appointed as a teacher and Minister of Education; teaching middle school in the cities of Hail and Buraydah. In 1967, he moved to Riyadh to perform the same job. He enrolled in the Higher Judicial Institute and earned his Master's degree in Comparative Jurisprudence in the year

1979. He began teaching high school in the year 1983 and remained in this position until he retired due to health reasons.

He would worship a great deal; to include praying, fasting and supplicating. He loved knowledge, reviewing and studying. He spent his time in beneficial matters. He was humble and always smiling; and also patient and generous with the needy and elderly. He spent his time, efforts and money in *dawah* to the path of Allāh ﷻ.

He passed away in Mecca in the year 1994, during the month of Ramaḍān.

Shaykh 'Abdullāh ibn Jāru Allāh authored over 150 written works. Most of them are small concise works dealing with the major needs of the general Muslims.

TRANSLATOR'S INTRODUCTION

All praises belong to Allāh, the Lord of all that exists, the Most Beneficent and the Most Merciful of those who show mercy. May Allāh exalt the rank of and send peace upon the best of mankind, Muḥammad ibn 'Abdullāh, and upon his family and his companions collectively. As to what follows:

The intent of this translation is to provide the English speaker with an authentic book concerning dream interpretation. As for the popular English books *Islamic Dream Interpretations* by Muḥammad Ibn Sireen and *Ibn Seerin's Dictionary Of Dreams,* these books are not by Ibn Sireen.

Questioner: Noble Shaykh, the questioner asks about the books of Ibn Sireen. Did Ibn Sireen specialize in dream interpretation? And can it be said that the books present now in the libraries and bookstores are by Ibn Sireen?

Shaykh Fawzān: This is a lie. Ibn Sireen does not have any books about dream interpretation. This book which is present now is not by Ibn Sireen; rather, it was falsely attributed to him.

Rasheed ibn Estes Barbee

Durham, North Carolina

Rajab 1441/March 2020

INTRODUCTION OF SHAYKH ‘ABDULLĀH JĀRU ALLĀH

In the Name of Allāh, the Most Beneficent and the Most Merciful of those who show mercy. All praises belong to Allāh, the Lord of all that exists. I bear witness that nothing has the right to be worshipped except for Allāh alone without partners; and I bear witness that Muḥammad is His slave and Messenger. May Allāh exalt his rank and send peace upon him, and upon his family and his companions collectively. As to what follows:

Indeed dream interpretation is a great important knowledge that appears in the Glorious Qur'ān and the pure Sunnah. It is built upon correct understanding; interpreting the speech, perception and morale. It is based on what is appropriate as it relates to the situation of the dreamer, the time in which the dream occurs, and the matters connected to the dream.

Allāh ﷻ complimented Yūsuf ibn Ya‘qūb ﷺ for his knowledge of dream interpretation in accordance with the legislation and the rulings connected to them.

﴿ وَكَذَٰلِكَ يَجْتَبِيكَ رَبُّكَ وَيُعَلِّمُكَ مِن تَأْوِيلِ الْأَحَادِيثِ وَيُتِمُّ نِعْمَتَهُ عَلَيْكَ وَعَلَىٰ آلِ يَعْقُوبَ كَمَا أَتَمَّهَا عَلَىٰ أَبَوَيْكَ مِن قَبْلُ إِبْرَاهِيمَ وَإِسْحَاقَ ۚ إِنَّ رَبَّكَ عَلِيمٌ حَكِيمٌ ﴿٦﴾ ﴾

Thus will your Lord choose you and teach you the interpretation of dreams (and other things) and perfect His favor on you and on the offspring of Ya'qūb, as He perfected it on your fathers, 'Ibrāhīm and Isḥāq aforetime! Verily, your Lord is All-Knowing, All-Wise.[1]

There is a difference between this and those dreams that have no interpretation; like what someone sees in a dream from the matters he has spent long hours pondering over. Indeed, much of what people see in their sleep is based upon what they ponder over while they are awake.

This category of dreams, in most cases, is called "confused dreams". This type of dream has no interpretation. Another type of dream is that which Satan places upon the soul of the sleeper. These are false dreams with misunderstood meanings. These dreams, likewise, have no interpretation; and the intelligent person should not busy himself thinking about these dreams.

As for the authentic dreams, they are inspiration that Allāh ﷻ inspires the soul with during its separation from the body at the time of sleep. These are examples given to the person so he may understand that which is relevant to him.

[1] Sūrah Yūsuf 12:6

Due to the importance of dream interpretation in the life of the individual, I compiled within this treatise etiquettes extracted from the Noble Qur'ān and pure Sunnah, connected to the etiquettes of righteous dreams and nightmares.

I ask Allāh, the Exalted, to benefit us with it and may Allāh exalt the rank of Prophet Muḥammad ﷺ and send peace upon him and upon his family and his companions collectively.

CHAPTER *One*

Types of Dreams

Truthful Dreams

Allāh, ﷻ, said:

﴿ وَمِنْ آيَاتِهِ مَنَامُكُم بِاللَّيْلِ وَالنَّهَارِ ﴿٢٣﴾ ﴾

And among His Signs is the sleep that you take by night and by day.[1]

[1] Sūrah Ar-Rūm 30:23

From His signs that prove His power and manifest His divinity and oneness are your dreams and sleep. That is because the person loses perception such that the sleeping person becomes like the deceased person; then he awakens, and his perception returns to him. This is proof of the power of Allāh ﷻ.

'Abū Huraira ؓ said: "I heard the Messenger of Allāh ﷺ say:

لَمْ يَبْقَ مِنَ النُّبُوَّةِ إِلاَّ الْمُبَشِّرَاتُ ". قَالُوا وَمَا الْمُبَشِّرَاتُ قَالَ " الرُّؤْيَا الصَّالِحَةُ

Nothing remains of prophecy except for glad tidings. They said: And what are glad tidings? He said: Truthful righteous dreams.[1]

Explanation of the Ḥadīth

This *ḥadīth* shows that there are some dreams that are true, and Allāh ﷻ reveals to the believer what will occur from good or evil. Although, in this narration he only mentions the glad tidings because this is what occurs most often; as opposed to giving the believer warnings. And there is no revelation after the death of the Prophet ﷺ.

'Abū Huraira ؓ said the Prophet ﷺ said:

إِذَا اقْتَرَبَ الزَّمَانُ لَمْ تَكَدْ رُؤْيَا الْمُؤْمِنِ تَكْذِبُ وَأَصْدَقُهُمْ رُؤْيَا أَصْدَقُهُمْ حَدِيثًا وَرُؤْيَا الْمُسْلِمِ جُزْءٌ مِنْ سِتَّةٍ وَأَرْبَعِينَ جُزْءًا مِنَ النُّبُوَّةِ

When the end of time comes near, the dream of the believer will rarely be false. The most truthful of them in dream will be the most truthful in speech. The dream of a Muslim is one part of forty-six parts of prophecy.[2]

---

[1] Ṣaḥīḥ al-Bukhārī 6990

[2] Jāmiʿ at-Tirmidhī 2439

Explanation of the Ḥadīth

Indeed, Allāh ﷻ gives solace to the believer and comfort by the true dreams He shows him; as this occurs during the era of trials and tribulations. The truthfulness of the dream increases based upon the truthfulness of the speech of the individual.

Al-Muhallab[1] said: The dreams of the Prophets are the truth, while the dreams of the believers are mostly correct due to the inability of Shayṭān to gain mastery over their hearts. The dreams of the sinners and disbelievers are mostly false, due to the mastery Shayṭān has over their souls. The truthful dream is a part of prophecy, as Allāh ﷻ reveals to some believers while they are sleeping. The statement "when the end of time comes near" means when the duration of the world comes to an end.

Seeing the Prophet ﷺ

'Abū Huraira ؓ said the Messenger of Allāh ﷺ said:

مَنْ رَآنِي فِي الْمَنَامِ فَسَيَرَانِي فِي الْيَقَظَةِ أَوْ لَكَأَنَّمَا رَآنِي فِي الْيَقَظَةِ لاَ يَتَمَثَّلُ الشَّيْطَانُ بِي

Whoever sees me in a dream, then he will see me while he is awake (or he said it is as though he has seen me while awake). Shayṭān cannot appear in my form.[2]

Explanation of the Ḥadīth

The meaning of "Whoever sees me in a dream, then he will see me while he is awake" is that he will see the affirmation of seeing him ﷺ

[1] Al-Muhallab ibn Aḥmad ibn 'Abī Ṣufrah died 435 years after the migration.

[2] Ṣaḥīḥ Muslim 2266

while he is awake. Those who see the Prophet ﷺ in a dream will see him while they are awake on the Day of Judgement. This is a glad tiding for the person who has this dream. Therefore, it is as though he has seen him while awake, and this is a glad tiding that indicates nobility for the person who has this dream. No one will see the Messenger of Allāh ﷺ in a dream except for the person with love in his heart for him and those who adhere to his guidance. Seeing the Prophet ﷺ in a dream is true; and it is not from the confused, muddled dreams because Shayṭān cannot appear to the people in the form of the Prophet ﷺ. This is something which is specific to the Prophet ﷺ.

Good and Hated Dreams

'Abū Sa'id al-Khudrī said: I heard the Prophet ﷺ saying:

إِذَا رَأَى أَحَدُكُمْ رُؤْيَا يُحِبُّهَا فَإِنَّمَا هِيَ مِنَ اللَّهِ، فَلْيَحْمَدِ اللَّهَ عَلَيْهَا، وَلْيُحَدِّثْ بِهَا، وَإِذَا رَأَى غَيْرَ ذَلِكَ مِمَّا يَكْرَهُ، فَإِنَّمَا هِيَ مِنَ الشَّيْطَانِ، فَلْيَسْتَعِذْ مِنْ شَرِّهَا، وَلاَ يَذْكُرْهَا لأَحَدٍ، فَإِنَّهَا لاَ تَضُرُّهُ

If one of you sees a dream that he loves then indeed it is from Allāh, thus praise Allāh for it and narrate it. And if he sees that which he hates, then indeed it is from Shayṭān. Thus seek refuge from its evil and do not mention it to anyone, then indeed it will not harm him.[1]

Explanation of the Ḥadīth

When the person sees a good dream, then he attributes it to Allāh and he praises Allāh for seeing that which makes him happy. There is nothing wrong if he mentions his dream because it brings about optimism, and optimism is something which is sought after. And if he sees

[1] Ṣaḥīḥ al-Bukhārī 6985

an evil dream, then he attributes it to Shayṭān, because in most cases it is from the whispers of Shayṭān. He should not speak to anyone about it because this brings about pessimism, and pessimism is prohibited. Therefore, seek refuge with Allāh ﷻ; place your trust in Him, and the dream will not cause any harm.

'Abū Qatādah ﷺ said the Prophet ﷺ said:

الرُّؤْيَا الصَّالِحَةُ مِنَ اللَّهِ، وَالْحُلْمُ مِنَ الشَّيْطَانِ، فَإِذَا حَلَمَ فَلْيَتَعَوَّذْ مِنْهُ وَلْيَبْصُقْ عَنْ شِمَالِهِ، فَإِنَّهَا لاَ تَضُرُّهُ

The good dream is from Allāh, while the nightmare is from Shayṭān. Thus, whoever has a nightmare, then let him seek refuge from it and spit on his left side, then indeed it will not harm him.[1]

Explanation of the Ḥadīth

The terms *al-rūyā* and *al-ḥulm* both mean dream in the origin of the words. As for the Islamic meaning, then *al-rūyā* refers to a good dream, while *al-ḥulm* refers to an evil dream. It is recommended to spit on the left side and seek refuge from Shayṭān upon seeing an evil dream. This is spittle with no saliva. That repels the Shayṭān and belittles him. Likewise, the person should not pay attention to the images he saw, because the whispers of Shayṭān cannot harm anyone except by the permission of Allāh ﷻ.

Jabir ﷺ said the Messenger of Allāh ﷺ said:

إِذَا رَأَى أَحَدُكُمُ الرُّؤْيَا يَكْرَهُهَا فَلْيَبْصُقْ عَنْ يَسَارِهِ ثَلاَثًا وَلْيَسْتَعِذْ بِاللَّهِ مِنَ الشَّيْطَانِ ثَلاَثًا وَلْيَتَحَوَّلْ عَنْ جَنْبِهِ الَّذِي كَانَ عَلَيْهِ

[1] Ṣaḥīḥ al-Bukhārī 6986

If one of you sees a dream he hates, then let him spit to his left side three times, and let him seek refuge with Allāh from Shayṭān three times, and let him alternate the side he was lying on.[1]

Explanation of the Ḥadīth

It is recommended to lie on a different side than the person was lying on when he saw the hated dream. The left side is specified with light spittle because this is the side of Shayṭān.

Falsifying Dreams

Wāthila bin al-Asqa'i ﷺ said the Messenger of Allāh ﷺ said:

إِنَّ مِنْ أَعْظَمِ الْفِرَى أَنْ يَدَّعِيَ الرَّجُلُ إِلَى غَيْرِ أَبِيهِ، أَوْ يُرِيَ عَيْنَهُ مَا لَمْ تَرَ، أَوْ يَقُولُ عَلَى رَسُولِ اللَّهِ صلى الله عليه وسلم مَا لَمْ يَقُلْ

Indeed from the worst lies is to claim falsely to be the son of someone other than one's real father, or to claim to have had a dream one has not had, or to attribute to me what I have not said.[2]

Explanation of the Ḥadīth

To falsely claim lineage to other than one's actual father is a major sin because it causes the true lineage to be lost, and enters into the family those who are not from the family; along with many other matters prohibited from the legislation. Lying about a dream is a major sin because it is lying against Allāh ﷻ, claiming that Allāh showed the person something, while indeed He did not show this to him. This is in contrast to

[1] Ṣaḥīḥ Muslim 2262
[2] Ṣaḥīḥ al-Bukhārī 3509

the person who lies about seeing something while awake, because in this case he lies against the creation. Therefore, although lying about something that occurred while awake is impermissible, it is a lesser sin that to lie about a dream, because lying about a dream is to lie against Allāh ﷻ. Lying against the Messenger of Allāh ﷺ is also a major sin due to what it results in from misleading the people concerning the religion.

Narrating Good Dreams

Imām 'Abdur Raḥman as-Sa'dī رحمه الله said:

'Abū Qatādah رضي الله عنه said the Messenger of Allāh ﷺ said:

الرُّؤْيَا الْحَسَنَةُ مِنَ اللَّهِ، فَإِذَا رَأَى أَحَدُكُمْ مَا يُحِبُّ فَلاَ يُحَدِّثْ بِهِ إِلاَّ مَنْ يُحِبُّ، وَإِذَا رَأَى مَا يَكْرَهُ فَلْيَتَعَوَّذْ بِاللَّهِ مِنْ شَرِّهَا، وَمِنْ شَرِّ الشَّيْطَانِ وَلْيَتْفِلْ ثَلاَثًا وَلاَ يُحَدِّثْ بِهَا أَحَدًا فَإِنَّهَا لَنْ تَضُرَّهُ

The good dream is from Allāh, thus if one of you see that which he loves then do not inform anyone except those he loves. And if he sees that which he hates, then seek refuge with Allāh from its evil, and from the evil of Shayṭān, and spit lightly three times, and do not narrate it to anyone, and then it will not cause any harm.[1]

Explanation of the Ḥadīth

The righteous dream is from Allāh ﷻ, meaning it is safe from the confusion of Shayṭān and his disruption. When the person goes to sleep, his soul leaves his body and it experiences some foreshadowing which has been gathered from many sciences of knowledge. Allāh ﷻ inspires it and the angel brings it to him while he is sleeping. The dream gives him

[1] Ṣaḥīḥ al-Bukhārī 7044

warnings and alerts him to matters of which he was previously ignorant, or reminds him of matters of which he was heedless. The dream may inform him of matters that will benefit him or caution him from matters that will harm his religion or worldly life; matters that he had not given any thought previously. The dream may increase his zeal toward any action that was hidden from him; or alert him to some specific details. These are all signs of a righteous dream which is one part from 46 parts of prophecy. And that which is from prophecy is not false.

Look at the dream of the Prophet ﷺ in the statement of Allāh ﷻ.

﴿ إِذْ يُرِيكَهُمُ اللَّهُ فِي مَنَامِكَ قَلِيلًا ۖ وَلَوْ أَرَاكَهُمْ كَثِيرًا لَّفَشِلْتُمْ وَلَتَنَازَعْتُمْ فِي الْأَمْرِ وَلَٰكِنَّ اللَّهَ سَلَّمَ ۗ إِنَّهُ عَلِيمٌ بِذَاتِ الصُّدُورِ ﴿٤٣﴾ ﴾

(And remember) when Allāh showed them to you as few in your dream, if He had shown them to you as many, you would surely have been discouraged, and you would surely have disputed in making a decision. But Allāh saved you. Certainly, He is the All-Knower of what is in the breasts.[1]

How much benefit was attained by way of this dream, and how much harm was prevented!

Likewise, the statement of Allāh ﷻ:

[1] Sūrah al-'Anfāl 8:43

﴿ لَّقَدْ صَدَقَ اللَّهُ رَسُولَهُ الرُّؤْيَا بِالْحَقِّ ۖ لَتَدْخُلُنَّ الْمَسْجِدَ الْحَرَامَ إِن شَاءَ اللَّهُ آمِنِينَ مُحَلِّقِينَ رُءُوسَكُمْ وَمُقَصِّرِينَ لَا تَخَافُونَ ۖ فَعَلِمَ مَا لَمْ تَعْلَمُوا فَجَعَلَ مِن دُونِ ذَٰلِكَ فَتْحًا قَرِيبًا ﴿٢٧﴾ ﴾

Indeed, Allāh shall fulfil the true vision which He showed to His Messenger in truth. Certainly, you shall enter Al-Masjid-al-Ḥarām if Allāh wills, secure, some having your heads shaved, and some having your head hair cut short, having no fear. He knew what you knew not, and He granted besides that a near victory.[1]

This dream increased their faith, and completed their certainty, and this was a great sign from Allāh ﷻ.

Look at the dream of the king of Egypt, and the truthful interpretation of Yūsūf ﵇.

﴿ وَقَالَ الْمَلِكُ إِنِّي أَرَىٰ سَبْعَ بَقَرَاتٍ سِمَانٍ يَأْكُلُهُنَّ سَبْعٌ عِجَافٌ وَسَبْعَ سُنبُلَاتٍ خُضْرٍ وَأُخَرَ يَابِسَاتٍ ۖ يَا أَيُّهَا الْمَلَأُ أَفْتُونِي فِي رُؤْيَايَ إِن كُنتُمْ لِلرُّؤْيَا تَعْبُرُونَ ﴿٤٣﴾ ﴾

And the king (of Egypt) said: "Verily, I saw (in a dream) seven fat cows, whom seven lean ones were devouring—and of seven green ears of corn and (seven) others dry. O notables! Explain to me my dream, if it be that you can interpret dreams."[2]

---

[1] Sūrah al-Fatḥ 48:27
[2] Sūrah Yūsūf 12:43

﴿ يُوسُفُ أَيُّهَا الصِّدِّيقُ أَفْتِنَا فِي سَبْعِ بَقَرَاتٍ سِمَانٍ يَأْكُلُهُنَّ سَبْعٌ عِجَافٌ وَسَبْعِ
سُنبُلَاتٍ خُضْرٍ وَأُخَرَ يَابِسَاتٍ لَّعَلِّي أَرْجِعُ إِلَى النَّاسِ لَعَلَّهُمْ يَعْلَمُونَ ﴿٤٦﴾ ﴾

(He said): "O Yūsūf, the man of truth! Explain to us (the dream) of seven fat cows whom seven lean ones were devouring, and of seven green ears of corn, and (seven) others dry, that I may return to the people, and that they may know."[1]

﴿ قَالَ تَزْرَعُونَ سَبْعَ سِنِينَ دَأَبًا فَمَا حَصَدتُّمْ فَذَرُوهُ فِي سُنبُلِهِ إِلَّا قَلِيلًا مِّمَّا تَأْكُلُونَ
﴿٤٧﴾ ثُمَّ يَأْتِي مِن بَعْدِ ذَٰلِكَ سَبْعٌ شِدَادٌ يَأْكُلْنَ مَا قَدَّمْتُمْ لَهُنَّ إِلَّا قَلِيلًا مِّمَّا تُحْصِنُونَ
﴿٤٨﴾ ثُمَّ يَأْتِي مِن بَعْدِ ذَٰلِكَ عَامٌ فِيهِ يُغَاثُ النَّاسُ وَفِيهِ يَعْصِرُونَ ﴿٤٩﴾ ﴾

(Yūsūf) said: "For seven consecutive years, you shall sow as usual and that (the harvest) which you reap you shall leave in ears, (all) except a little of it which you may eat. Then will come after that seven difficult [years] which will consume what you saved for them, except a little from which you will store. Then will come after that a year in which the people will be given rain and in which they will press [olives and grapes]."[2]

Just as he was entrusted to interpret the dreams, Allāh ﷻ placed him over the affairs of government explained within them. Thus, a great deal of good was achieved by way of this, harm was repelled, and Allāh ﷻ elevated the status of Yūsūf above of His slaves.

---

[1] Sūrah Yūsūf 12:46

[2] Sūrah Yūsūf 12:47-49

﴿ قَالَ اجْعَلْنِي عَلَىٰ خَزَائِنِ الْأَرْضِ ۖ إِنِّي حَفِيظٌ عَلِيمٌ ﴿٥٥﴾ وَكَذَٰلِكَ مَكَّنَّا لِيُوسُفَ فِي الْأَرْضِ يَتَبَوَّأُ مِنْهَا حَيْثُ يَشَاءُ ۚ نُصِيبُ بِرَحْمَتِنَا مَن نَّشَاءُ ۖ وَلَا نُضِيعُ أَجْرَ الْمُحْسِنِينَ ﴿٥٦﴾ ﴾

(Yūsūf) said: "Set me over the storehouses of the land; I will indeed guard them with full knowledge" And thus We established Yūsūf in the land to settle therein wherever he willed. We touch with Our mercy whom We will, and We do not allow to be lost the reward of those who do good.[1]

Reflect over the dream of 'Abdullāh ibn Zayd and 'Umār ibn al-Khaṭṭāb concerning the *adhān* and *'iqāmah*, and how it became a source of legislation for this great rite which is from the greatest rites of Islām.

'Abdullāh ibn Zayd said: "There appeared to me in a dream a man who was wearing two green garments, in whose hand was a bell. I said, 'O slave of Allāh, will you sell that bell?' He said, 'What will you do with it?' I said, 'We will call the people to prayer with it.' He said, 'Shall I not show you something better than that?' I said, 'Yes.' He said, 'Say, Allāhu akbar, Allāhu akbar ... (to the end of the *adhān*).' When morning came, I went to the Messenger of Allāh ﷺ and told him what I had seen. He said, 'This is a true dream, insha Allāh. Go to Bilāl and tell him what you have seen so that he can give the call, because he has a more beautiful voice than you.' So I went to Bilāl and started telling him what I had seen, and he gave the call to prayer. 'Umār ibn al-Khaṭṭāb heard that while he was in his house, and he came out dragging his cloak behind

---

[1] Sūrah Yūsūf 12:55-56

him, saying, 'By the One Who sent you with the truth, O Messenger of Allāh, I saw the same as he saw.' The Messenger of Allāh ﷺ said: 'All praises belong to Allāh.'"[1]

One cannot enumerate the benefits contained in the dreams of the Prophets, allies of Allāh ﷻ, righteous people; rather, even the general believers. They are from the favors of Allāh ﷻ upon His slaves. They are glad tidings for the believers, warnings for the heedless, a reminder for those who turned away, and an argument against the obstinate.

As for nightmares, they are the muddled dreams from Shayṭān upon the soul of the person. He shows him confusing matters that will frighten him and bring about things that will cause him grief and worry. Or he shows him that which will cause him to be prideful, conceited or arrogant. Or he will scare the soul to bring about evil, corruption or harm. In the event this occurs, the Prophet ﷺ ordered the person to take means to repel the evil of Shayṭān, which is to spit lightly three times to the left side; and he ﷺ ordered the individual to not narrate it to anyone. These are means to exterminate and invalidate the dream. The person should also seek refuge with Allāh ﷻ from the accursed Shayṭān, as he is the reason for this nightmare. This will repel the hated dream and bring ease to the heart, and the dream will cause no harm. By doing this, we believe the statement of the Messenger ﷺ and we trust these means will be successful.

As for the good dreams, it is befitting to praise Allāh ﷻ for them and to ask Him to actualize them. But you should only narrate them to those you love and those that love you. This is to bring them happiness and so they will supplicate for you. Do not narrate good dreams to those you

---

[1] Aḥmad 1588, 'Abū Dāwūd 421 & 430, Ibn Mājah 698

do not love. This is so they will not give you a confused interpretation that agrees with their desires or become envious of you and hope that the blessings are removed from you.

For this reason, when Yūsūf saw in a dream the sun, moon and eleven stars prostrating to him, and he narrated this dream to his father, his father said to him:

﴿ قَالَ يَا بُنَيَّ لَا تَقْصُصْ رُؤْيَاكَ عَلَىٰ إِخْوَتِكَ فَيَكِيدُوا لَكَ كَيْدًا ۖ إِنَّ الشَّيْطَانَ لِلْإِنسَانِ عَدُوٌّ مُّبِينٌ ﴿٥﴾ ﴾

He said: O my dear son, relate not your vision to your brothers, lest they arrange a plot against you. Verily Shayṭān is to man an open enemy![1]

Thus, it is preferred to conceal blessings from the enemy as much as possible, unless there is a benefit that outweighs the harm.

Know, a righteous dream may sometimes be seen by the person in the form of an external image, as in the case of the dream about the *adhān*. Sometimes the person will be shown tangible examples so he can consider them based upon normal affairs that occur, as in the case of the dream of the king of Egypt. The vision shown will vary based upon the person who is dreaming, the time of the dream, the habits of the person, and their various situations.[2]

---

[1] Sūrah Yūsūf 12:5

[2] *Joy to the Hearts of the Pious, and Delight to the Eyes of the Righteous* by Shaykh 'Abdur Raḥman as-Sā'di, pages 171-174

Etiquettes for Good Dreams

When a person sees a good dream, it is recommended that he does three things.

- He should praise Allāh ﷻ for the dream
- He should view it as glad tidings
- He should only narrate the dream to those he loves and should not tell those he does not love.

'Abū Sa'īd al-Khudrī ﷺ said, "I heard the Prophet saying:

إِذَا رَأَى أَحَدُكُمْ رُؤْيَا يُحِبُّهَا فَإِنَّمَا هِيَ مِنَ اللَّهِ، فَلْيَحْمَدِ اللَّهَ عَلَيْهَا، وَلْيُحَدِّثْ بِهَا، وَإِذَا رَأَى غَيْرَ ذَلِكَ مِمَّا يَكْرَهُ، فَإِنَّمَا هِيَ مِنَ الشَّيْطَانِ، فَلْيَسْتَعِذْ مِنْ شَرِّهَا، وَلاَ يَذْكُرْهَا لأَحَدٍ، فَإِنَّهَا لاَ تَضُرُّهُ

'If one of you sees a dream that he loves, then indeed it is from Allāh. Thus, praise Allāh for it and narrate it. And if he sees that which he hates, then indeed it is from Shayṭān. Thus, seek refuge from its evil and do not mention it to anyone. Then indeed it will not harm him.'"[1]

In the narration collected in Ṣaḥīḥ Muslim:

'Abū Qatādah ﷺ said the Messenger of Allāh ﷺ said:

الرُّؤْيَا الْحَسَنَةُ مِنَ اللَّهِ، فَإِذَا رَأَى أَحَدُكُمْ مَا يُحِبُّ فَلاَ يُحَدِّثْ بِهِ إِلاَّ مَنْ يُحِبُّ

The good dream is from Allāh. Thus, if one of you see that which he loves, then do not inform anyone except those he loves.[2]

[1] Ṣaḥīḥ al-Bukhārī 6985

[2] Ṣaḥīḥ al-Bukhārī 7044

Etiquettes for Nightmares

'Abū Salamah said:

لَقَدْ كُنْتُ أَرَى الرُّؤْيَا فَتُمْرِضُنِي حَتَّى سَمِعْتُ أَبَا قَتَادَةَ يَقُولُ وَأَنَا كُنْتُ لأَرَى الرُّؤْيَا تُمْرِضُنِي، حَتَّى سَمِعْتُ النَّبِيَّ صلى الله عليه وسلم يَقُولُ " الرُّؤْيَا الْحَسَنَةُ مِنَ اللَّهِ، فَإِذَا رَأَى أَحَدُكُمْ مَا يُحِبُّ فَلاَ يُحَدِّثْ بِهِ إِلاَّ مَنْ يُحِبُّ، وَإِذَا رَأَى مَا يَكْرَهُ فَلْيَتَعَوَّذْ بِاللَّهِ مِنْ شَرِّهَا، وَمِنْ شَرِّ الشَّيْطَانِ وَلْيَتْفِلْ ثَلاَثًا وَلاَ يُحَدِّثْ بِهَا أَحَدًا فَإِنَّهَا لَنْ تَضُرَّهُ

I used to see a dream which would make me sick, until I heard 'Abū Qatāda saying: "I too, used to see a dream which would make me sick, until I heard the Prophet ﷺ saying: 'A good dream is from Allāh, so if anyone of you saw a dream which he liked, he should not tell it to anybody except to the one whom he loves; and if he saw a dream which he disliked, then he should seek refuge with Allāh from its evil and from the evil of Shayṭān, and spit three times (on his left) and should not tell it to anybody, for it will not harm him.'"[1]

Jābir ﷺ said the Messenger of Allāh ﷺ said:

إِذَا رَأَى أَحَدُكُمُ الرُّؤْيَا يَكْرَهُهَا فَلْيَبْصُقْ عَنْ يَسَارِهِ ثَلاَثًا وَلْيَسْتَعِذْ بِاللَّهِ مِنَ الشَّيْطَانِ ثَلاَثًا وَلْيَتَحَوَّلْ عَنْ جَنْبِهِ الَّذِي كَانَ عَلَيْهِ

If one of you sees a dream he hates, then let him spit to his left side three times and let him seek refuge with Allāh from Shayṭān three times; and let him alternate the side he was lying on.[2]

[1] Ṣaḥīḥ al-Bukhārī 7044
[2] Ṣaḥīḥ Muslim 2262

'Abū Huraira ﷺ said the Prophet ﷺ said:

إِذَا اقْتَرَبَ الزَّمَانُ لَمْ تَكَدْ رُؤْيَا الْمُؤْمِنِ تَكْذِبُ وَأَصْدَقُهُمْ رُؤْيَا أَصْدَقُهُمْ حَدِيثًا وَرُؤْيَا الْمُسْلِمِ جُزْءٌ مِنْ سِتَّةٍ وَأَرْبَعِينَ جُزْءًا مِنَ النُّبُوَّةِ

When the end of time comes near, the dream of the believer will rarely be false. The most truthful of them in dream will be the most truthful in speech. The dream of a Muslim is one part of 46 parts of prophecy.[1]

Six Things to Do After Having a Nightmare

There are six steps the person should take after seeing a dream he hates.

- Seek refuge with Allāh ﷻ from its evil; and this is prescribed for the believer to do for every affair that he hates.
- Seek refuge with Allāh ﷻ from Shayṭān, because this dream is from Shayṭān. He shows the person nightmares to cause man sadness and to intimidate him about the future.
- Spit lightly on the left side to repel the Shayṭān, the one who has brought this hated dream. This is to belittle him and recognize him as impure. The left side is specified because it is the place of filth. And the person spits three times to affirm it.
- Alternate the side you were sleeping on; and perhaps this is done to bring about optimism so the person can change his situation. And Allāh ﷻ knows best.

---

[1] Jāmiʿ at-Tirmidhī 2439

- The person should get up and pray. This is because praying is turning to Allāh ﷻ and seeking refuge with Him, and protection from the evil one. By praying, the person perfects what he is seeking due to his closeness to his Lord while his is in prostration.
- He should not narrate his nightmare to anyone, and he should not explain it himself; because dreams occur according to how they are explained. Also, he should not narrate it so it will not have a negative effect upon his soul.[1]

Dreams Come to Pass According to How They Are Interpreted

'Anas ﷺ said the Messenger of Allāh ﷺ said:

إنَّ الرُّؤْيا تَقَعُ على ما تُعَبَّرُ ، و مَثَلُ ذلِكَ مَثَلُ رجلٍ رفعَ رِجلَيْهِ فهو يَنتظِرُ متَى يَضعُها، فإذا رأَى أحدُكمْ رُؤْيا فلا يُحَدِّثْ بِها إلا ناصِحًا أو عالِمًا

Indeed, the dream occurs as it is interpreted. The example of this is that of a man who lifts his feet while waiting to place them down. So if one of you sees a dream, do not narrate it to anyone except a good advisor or a scholar.[2]

'Abū Razīn said he heard the Prophet ﷺ say:

---

[1] From the explanation of Fatḥ al-Bārī 12/387-389
[2] Silsila Ṣaḥīḥ by al-Albanī 120

الرُّؤْيَا عَلَى رِجْلِ طَائِرٍ مَا لَمْ تُعْبَرْ فَإِذَا عُبِرَتْ وَقَعَتْ " . قَالَ " وَالرُّؤْيَا جُزْءٌ مِنْ سِتَّةٍ وَأَرْبَعِينَ جُزْءًا مِنَ النُّبُوَّةِ " . قَالَ وَأَحْسِبُهُ قَالَ " لاَ يَقُصُّهَا إِلاَّ عَلَى وَادٍّ أَوْ ذِي رَأْيٍ

"Dreams are attached to the foot of a bird until they are interpreted; then when they are interpreted they come to pass." He said: "And dreams are one of the 46 parts of prophecy." He (the narrator) said: "And I think he said: 'A person should not tell them except to one whom he loves or one who is wise.'"[1]

'Ā'ishah, the wife of the Prophet ﷺ, said: "There was a woman from the people of Madinah who was married to a merchant who would travel for business. Each time he would leave her to go out for trade, she would have a dream about him; and it was rare that he would go out for business except that she was pregnant. She came to the Messenger of Allāh ﷺ and said: 'My husband left to go out for trade and left me pregnant. I saw in a dream that the corridor of my home was broken, and I gave birth to a one-eyed male child.'

The Messenger of Allāh ﷺ said: 'Everything is fine. Your husband will return to you insha Allāh, well and good, and you will give birth to a righteous child.'

She saw the same dream two or three times, and each time she came to the Messenger of Allāh ﷺ and he would tell her the same thing, 'Your husband will return to you, and you will give birth to a righteous child insha Allāh.'

She returned to see him on the usual day that she would come, but the Messenger of Allāh ﷺ was absent. She had the same dream the previous

[1] Sunan Ibn Mājah 3914

night. So I said to her: 'What have you come to ask about?' She said: 'I came to ask the Messenger of Allāh ﷺ about my dream. Each time I come he says it will be fine and it occurs just as he says.' I said to her: 'Tell me about the dream.' She said: 'I will wait until the Messenger of Allāh ﷺ arrives so I can tell him as I have done in the past.'

By Allāh, I continued to ask her until she told me the dream. I said to her: 'By Allāh, if this is truly what you saw, your husband will indeed die and you will give birth to a wicked child.' So she sat down and cried.

When the Messenger of Allāh ﷺ arrived, he said: 'What is the matter with her, 'Ā'ishah?' And I informed him of what occurred, and the interpretation I gave her for her dream.' The Messenger of Allāh ﷺ said: 'Quiet O 'Ā'ishah, if you interpret for a Muslim his dream then interpret it with a good interpretation; for indeed the dreams will come to pass as they are interpreted by the person.' By Allāh, her husband died, and I saw that she gave birth to a wicked child."[1]

Sa'īd ibn Mansūr narrated that 'Aṭā'[2] used to say: "Dreams come to pass as they are interpreted."

These narrations are clear in explaining that dreams will occur in the manner in which they are explained. And it is possible to say that if Allāh ﷻ decrees for the dream to come to pass, then He will decree for the person to explain it in the manner in which it will occur. For this

---

[1] Collected by Ibn Hājr ibn al-Fatḥ al-Bārī 12/450

[2] Translator's note: He is 'Aṭā' ibn 'Abī Rabāḥ from the scholars of *tafsir* from the second generation. He was born in Yemen to Nubian African parents. He was the first Imām of Masjid al-Ḥarām in Mecca. He was a student of the great companion Ibn 'Abbās.

reason, the Messenger of Allāh ﷺ instructed us to only narrate our good dreams to a scholar or a good advisor, or to those we love or those with wisdom. And in another narration, he said "the intelligent person or those beloved to us."

Ibn al-'Arabī 'Abū Bakr al-Māliki[1] said: "As for the scholar, then he will give a good interpretation as much as is possible. As for the good advisor, then he will direct the person to that which will benefit him and assist him. As for the intelligent person, he will know the interpretation. He will know according to how the dream is explained to him, or he will remain silent. As for the person beloved to us, then he will know something good to say; and if he does not have something good to say he will remain silent."

There is no doubt that the interpretation of the dream is limited to what the dream actual contains; even if it is only from one standpoint, and it is not absolute from every standpoint. Imām al-Bukhārī alluded to this meaning in his chapter entitled, "Considering the Interpretation of a Dream Invalid If It Does Not Occur According to the First Intrepretation." He mentioned the narration of 'Abū Bakr ﷺ. Ibn 'Abbās ﷺ said:

---

[1] Translator's note: There are two well-known people known by the name "Ibn al-'Arabī". Muḥyi al-Dīn Ibn al-'Arabī was an extreme Sufi. While 'Abū Bakr ibn al-'Arabī al-Māliki was a noble scholar. Many scholars refer to the heretic Sufi as "Ibn 'Arabī" and the noble scholar as "Ibn al-'Arabī". Shaykh Ṣaliḥ Fawzān said: "Ibn 'Arabī was an apostate Sufi who claimed Allāh was one with His creation. While 'Abū Bakr ibn al-'Arabī al-Māliki was from our noble scholars, known for knowledge and piety. (*Al-Muntaqī min al-Fatāwā*, Shaykh Ṣaliḥ Fawzān, second volume, pages 306-307).

أَنَّ رَجُلاً أَتَى رَسُولَ اللَّهِ صلى الله عليه وسلم فَقَالَ إِنِّي رَأَيْتُ اللَّيْلَةَ فِي الْمَنَامِ ظُلَّةً تَنْطِفُ السَّمْنَ وَالْعَسَلَ، فَأَرَى النَّاسَ يَتَكَفَّفُونَ مِنْهَا فَالْمُسْتَكْثِرُ وَالْمُسْتَقِلُّ، وَإِذَا سَبَبٌ وَاصِلٌ مِنَ الأَرْضِ إِلَى السَّمَاءِ، فَأَرَاكَ أَخَذْتَ بِهِ فَعَلَوْتَ، ثُمَّ أَخَذَ بِهِ رَجُلٌ آخَرُ فَعَلاَ بِهِ، ثُمَّ أَخَذَ بِهِ رَجُلٌ آخَرُ فَعَلاَ بِهِ ثُمَّ أَخَذَ بِهِ رَجُلٌ آخَرُ فَانْقَطَعَ ثُمَّ وُصِلَ.

A man came to the Messenger of Allāh ﷺ and said, "I saw in a dream a cloud having shade. Butter and honey were dropping from it and I saw the people gathering it in their hands; some gathering much and some a little. And behold, there was a rope extending from the earth to the sky, and I saw that you (the Prophet) held it and went up, and then another man held it and went up and after that another held it and went up, and then after another man held it, but it broke and then got connected again."

فَقَالَ أَبُو بَكْرٍ يَا رَسُولَ اللَّهِ بِأَبِي أَنْتَ وَاللَّهِ لَتَدَعَنِّي فَأَعْبُرَهَا. فَقَالَ النَّبِيُّ صلى الله عليه وسلم " اعْبُرْ ".

'Abū Bakr said: "O Messenger of Allāh, may my father be sacrificed for you! Allow me to interpret this dream." The Prophet ﷺ said to him: "Interpret it."

قَالَ أَمَّا الظُّلَّةُ فَالإِسْلاَمُ، وَأَمَّا الَّذِي يَنْطِفُ مِنَ الْعَسَلِ وَالسَّمْنِ فَالْقُرْآنُ حَلاَوَتُهُ تَنْطُفُ، فَالْمُسْتَكْثِرُ مِنَ الْقُرْآنِ وَالْمُسْتَقِلُّ، وَأَمَّا السَّبَبُ الْوَاصِلُ مِنَ السَّمَاءِ إِلَى الأَرْضِ فَالْحَقُّ الَّذِي أَنْتَ عَلَيْهِ تَأْخُذُ بِهِ فَيُعْلِيكَ اللَّهُ، ثُمَّ يَأْخُذُ بِهِ رَجُلٌ مِنْ بَعْدِكَ فَيَعْلُو بِهِ، ثُمَّ يَأْخُذُ رَجُلٌ آخَرُ فَيَعْلُو بِهِ، ثُمَّ يَأْخُذُهُ رَجُلٌ آخَرُ فَيَنْقَطِعُ بِهِ ثُمَّ يُوَصَّلُ لَهُ فَيَعْلُو بِهِ،

'Abū Bakr said, "The cloud with shade symbolizes Islām, and the butter and honey dropping from it symbolizes the Qur'ān; its sweetness dropping and some people learning much of the Qur'ān, and some a little. The rope which is extended from the sky to the earth is the

Truth which you (the Prophet) are following. You follow it and Allāh will raise you high with it, and then another man will follow it and will rise up with it, and another person will follow it, and then another man will follow it but it will break, and then it will be connected for him and he will rise up with it.

فَأَخْبِرْنِي يَا رَسُولَ اللَّهِ بِأَبِي أَنْتَ أَصَبْتُ أَمْ أَخْطَأْتُ. قَالَ النَّبِيُّ صلى الله عليه وسلم " أَصَبْتَ بَعْضًا وَأَخْطَأْتَ بَعْضًا ".

Inform me, O Messenger of Allāh, may my father be sacrificed for you! Am I right or wrong?" The Prophet ﷺ replied, "You are right in some of it and wrong in some."

قَالَ فَوَاللَّهِ لَتُحَدِّثَنِّي بِالَّذِي أَخْطَأْتُ. قَالَ " لاَ تُقْسِمْ

'Abū Bakr said: "O Prophet of Allāh, I swear by Allāh, you must tell me in what I was wrong." The Prophet ﷺ said: "Do not swear."[1]

'Abū 'Ubaydah said: "The meaning of his statement, 'the dream is according to the first interpretation,' is if the first person to interpret the dream is a scholar; and thus he interprets the dream according to how it is to come to pass. Otherwise it can occur according to the interpretation of someone who correctly interprets it after him. This is because the occurrence of the dream only revolves around a correct interpretation that coincides with what Allāh ﷻ intended. Thus, when it occurs, it is not befitting to continue to ask others to interpret it. But if it does not occur, then another person can be asked. And he should inform the second person of what the first person was unaware.[2]

---

[1] Ṣaḥīḥ al-Bukhārī 7046
[2] Fatḥ al-Bārī 12/451

CHAPTER Two

Dream Interpretation Explained by Al-Baghawi

Dream Interpretation from the Qur'ān

Al-Baghawī[1] said: "Know the interpretation of dreams is divided into categories. Dreams can be explained with evidence from the Book of Allāh ﷻ, evidence from the Sunnah, or based upon proverbs found

[1] Translator's note: He is 'Abū Muḥammad al-Ḥusayn ibn Mas'ud ibn Muḥammad al-Farra' al-Baghawī. He was born around 433, after the migration. He is an Imām of *tafsir*. Shaykh Ṣaliḥ Fawzān said: "*Tafsir al-Baghawī* is a good condensed *tafsir* upon the methodology of the Salaf."

among the people. The interpretation may be interpreted according to names and meanings. And a dream may be interpreted with a meaning opposite to what the person saw.

Rope: A rope is interpreted as a covenant based upon the statement of Allāh ﷻ:

﴿ وَاعْتَصِمُوا بِحَبْلِ اللَّهِ جَمِيعًا ﴿١٠٣﴾ ﴾

And hold fast, all of you together.[1]

Ship: A ship is interpreted as safety based upon the statement of Allāh ﷻ:

﴿ فَأَنجَيْنَاهُ وَأَصْحَابَ السَّفِينَةِ ﴿١٥﴾ ﴾

Then We saved him and those with him in the ship.[2]

Wood: Wood is interpreted as hypocrisy based upon the statement of Allāh ﷻ:

﴿ كَأَنَّهُمْ خُشُبٌ مُّسَنَّدَةٌ ﴿٤﴾ ﴾

They are as blocks of wood propped up.[3]

Stones: Stones are interpreted as rigidness based upon the statement of Allāh ﷻ:

[1] Sūrah 'Āli 'Imrān 3:103
[2] Sūrah al-'Ankabūt 29:15
[3] Sūrah al-Munāfiqūn 63:4

﴿ فَهِيَ كَالْحِجَارَةِ أَوْ أَشَدُّ قَسْوَةً ﴿٧٤﴾ ﴾

Being like stones or even harder.[1]

Disease: Disease is interpreted as hypocrisy based upon the statement of Allāh ﷻ:

﴿ فِي قُلُوبِهِم مَّرَضٌ ﴿١٠﴾ ﴾

In their hearts is a disease.[2]

Egg: An egg is interpreted as women based upon the statement of Allāh ﷻ:

﴿ كَأَنَّهُنَّ بَيْضٌ مَّكْنُونٌ ﴿٤٩﴾ ﴾

As if they were [delicate] eggs, well-protected.[3]

Clothes: Clothes are interpreted as women based upon the statement of Allāh ﷻ:

﴿ هُنَّ لِبَاسٌ لَّكُمْ وَأَنتُمْ لِبَاسٌ لَّهُنَّ ﴿١٨٧﴾ ﴾

They are clothing for you, and you are clothing for them.[4]

---

[1] Sūrah al-Baqarah 2:74
[2] Sūrah al-Baqarah 2:10
[3] Sūrah aṣ-Ṣāffāt 37:49
[4] Sūrah al-Baqarah 2:187

Seeking victory: Seeking victory is interpreted as supplication based upon the statement of Allāh ﷻ:

﴿ إِن تَسْتَفْتِحُوا ﴿١٩﴾ ﴾

If you seek the victory.[1]

This means dū'ā'.

Water: Water is interpreted as a trial or tribulation.

﴿ لَأَسْقَيْنَاهُم مَّاءً غَدَقًا ﴿١٦﴾ لِّنَفْتِنَهُمْ فِيهِ ﴿١٧﴾ ﴾

We should surely have bestowed on them water (rain) in abundance. So We might test them therein.[2]

Eating raw meat: Eating raw meat is interpreted as backbiting based upon the statement of Allāh ﷻ:

﴿ أَيُحِبُّ أَحَدُكُمْ أَن يَأْكُلَ لَحْمَ أَخِيهِ مَيْتًا ﴿١٢﴾ ﴾

Would one of you like to eat the flesh of his dead brother?[3]

Entrance of a king: A king entering a place, a city, or a home by force—while the inhabitants hate that he should enter—is interpreted as a calamity that will afflict the people. This is based upon the statement of Allāh ﷻ:

---

[1] Sūrah al-'Anfāl 8:19

[2] Sūrah al-Jinn 72:16-17

[3] Sūrah al-Ḥujurāt 49:12

﴿ إِنَّ الْمُلُوكَ إِذَا دَخَلُوا قَرْيَةً أَفْسَدُوهَا ﴿٣٤﴾ ﴾

Indeed kings, when they enter a city, they ruin it.[1]

Dream Interpretation from the Sunnah

Crow: A crow is interpreted as a corrupt man based upon the statement of the Prophet ﷺ:

الْغُرَابُ فَاسِقٌ

The crow is corrupt.[2]

Mouse: A mouse is interpreted as a corrupt woman based upon the statement of the Prophet peace be upon him:

الْفَأْرَةُ فَاسِقَةٌ

The mouse is corrupt.[3]

Rib: The rib is interpreted as the woman based upon the statement of the Prophet ﷺ:

إِنَّ الْمَرْأَةَ خُلِقَتْ مِنْ ضِلَعٍ وَإِنَّ أَعْوَجَ شَىْءٍ فِي الضِّلَعِ أَعْلاَهُ

Indeed the woman is created from a rib, and the most crooked part of the rib is its top.[4]

---

[1] Sūrah an-Naml 27:34
[2] Sunan Ibn Mājah 3372
[3] Sunan Ibn Mājah 3372
[4] Ṣaḥīḥ Muslim 1468

Glass Vessels: Glass Vessels are interpreted as women based upon the statement of the Prophet ﷺ:

رُوَيْدَكَ يَا أَنْجَشَةُ، لاَ تَكْسِرِ الْقَوَارِيرَ

Slowly, O Anjasha![1] Do not break the glass vessels![2]

Dream Interpretation from the Proverbs of the People

Digging a hole: Digging a hole is interpreted as plotting based upon the proverb: "Whoever digs a hole will fall into it."

Allāh ﷻ said:

﴿ وَلَا يَحِيقُ الْمَكْرُ السَّيِّئُ إِلَّا بِأَهْلِهِ ﴿٤٣﴾ ﴾

But the evil plot encompasses only him who makes it.[3]

Collector of Firewood: A collector of firewood is interpreted as tale carrying based upon the proverb concerning those who carry tales: "Indeed he collects firewood."

Allāh ﷻ said:

﴿ وَامْرَأَتُهُ حَمَّالَةَ الْحَطَبِ ﴿٤﴾ ﴾

[1] Translator's note: Anjasha was a black camel herder from Abyssinia. His kunya was 'Abū Māriya. He was known for his beautiful voice. 'Anas ibn Mālik said: "Anjasha used to do the camel-chant for the women."

[2] Ṣaḥīḥ al-Bukhārī 6211

[3] Sūrah Fāṭir 35:43

And his wife too, who carries wood.[1]

This is because the wife of 'Abū Lahab used to slander the Prophet ﷺ.

Long hands: Long hands are interpreted as giving charity. This is based upon the proverb: "So and so has longer hands than them."

'Ā'ishah ﵂ said:

أَنَّ بَعْضَ، أَزْوَاجِ النَّبِيِّ صلى الله عليه وسلم قُلْنَ لِلنَّبِيِّ صلى الله عليه وسلم أَيُّنَا أَسْرَعُ بِكَ لُحُوقًا قَالَ " أَطْوَلُكُنَّ يَدًا ". فَأَخَذُوا قَصَبَةً يَذْرَعُونَهَا، فَكَانَتْ سَوْدَةُ أَطْوَلَهُنَّ يَدًا، فَعَلِمْنَا بَعْدُ أَنَّمَا كَانَتْ طُولَ يَدِهَا الصَّدَقَةُ، وَكَانَتْ أَسْرَعَنَا لُحُوقًا بِهِ وَكَانَتْ تُحِبُّ الصَّدَقَةَ

Some of the wives of the Prophet ﷺ asked him, "Who amongst us will be the first to follow you (die after you)?" He said, "Whoever has the longest hand." So they started measuring their hands with a stick and Sawdah had the longest hand. When Zainab bint Jaḥsh died first, we came to know that the long hand was a symbol of practicing charity; so she was the first to follow the Prophet ﷺ and she used to love to practice charity.[2]

Throwing stones or shooting arrows: Throwing stones or shooting arrows is interpreted as slander. This is based on the proverb: "Indecency was casted upon so and so."

Allāh ﷻ said:

﴿ وَالَّذِينَ يَرْمُونَ الْمُحْصَنَاتِ ﴿٤﴾ ﴾

---

[1] Sūrah al-Masad 111:4

[2] Ṣaḥīḥ al-Bukhārī 1420

And those who accuse chaste women[1]

Washing hands: Washing hands is interpreted as despair for hope based upon the proverb: "I have washed my hands of you."

Dream Interpretation According to Names

Dreams are also interpreted by names. For example, if someone sees a man name Rāshid (rightly-guided) it denotes guidance. If he sees a man named Sālim (safe) it denotes safety.

'Anas ibn Mālik said the Messenger of Allāh ﷺ said:

رَأَيْتُ ذَاتَ لَيْلَةٍ فِيمَا يَرَى النَّائِمُ كَأَنَّا فِي دَارِ عُقْبَةَ بْنِ رَافِعٍ فَأُتِينَا بِرُطَبٍ مِنْ رُطَبِ ابْنِ طَابٍ فَأَوَّلْتُ الرِّفْعَةَ لَنَا فِي الدُّنْيَا وَالْعَاقِبَةَ فِي الآخِرَةِ وَأَنَّ دِينَنَا قَدْ طَابَ

I saw during the night that which a person sees during sleep—as if we are in the house of 'Uqbah[2] ibn Rāfi'[3]—and there was brought to us the fresh dates of Ibn Ṭāb.[4] I interpreted it as the elevation for us in the world and a good ending in the Hereafter, and that our religion is good.[5]

Quince fruit: A quince fruit (السَّفَرْجَل) can mean travel if there is nothing in the dream that denotes sickness. This is because the name for this fruit begins with the same letters that mean travel (سفر).

---

[1] Sūrah an-Nūr 24:4

[2] Translator's note: 'Uqbah meaning "ending"

[3] Translator's note: Rāfi' meaning "elevation"

[4] Translator's note: Ṭāb meaning 'good'

[5] Ṣaḥīḥ Muslim 2270

Date stone: A date stone (نوى التمر) can mean the person intends to travel, because the word for date stone begins with the letters that mean "intention" (نوى).

Licorice: Licorice (السوس) can mean evil because the word for licorice begins with the same letters that mean evil (سوء).

Dream Interpretation According to Meaning

Citron fruit: The citron fruit can mean hypocrisy due to its inside being different from its outside. This is unless there is something within the dream that alludes to wealth.

Roses and Daffodils: Roses and daffodils can be interpreted as a short stay due to the quick manner in which roses and daffodils die.

Myrtle shrub: The myrtle evergreen shrub is interpreted as something remaining, because it remains green. It was narrated that a woman said: "I saw in a dream that my husband gave me daffodils and he gave my co-wife a myrtle shrub." It was said to her: "He will divorce you and keep your co-wife. Have you not heard the statement of the poet: 'There is no covenant for daffodils; the covenant only belongs to the myrtle.'"

Dream Interpretation According to the Opposite

Fear: Fear in a dream means safety. This is based on the statement of Allāh ﷻ:

﴿ وَلَيُبَدِّلَنَّهُم مِّن بَعْدِ خَوْفِهِمْ أَمْنًا ﴿٥٥﴾ ﴾

And He will surely give them in exchange a safe security after their fear.[1]

Safety in a dream means fear.

Crying is interpreted as happiness if it is not accompanied with screaming.

Laughing is interpreted as sadness unless the person is smiling.

Plague is interpreted as war. **War** is interpreted as the plague.

Hastiness in a matter is interpreted as regret. **Regret** is interpreted as hastiness.

Infatuation is interpreted as insanity. **Insanity** is interpreted as infatuation.

Marriage is interpreted a trade and trade is interpreted as marriage.

Cupping is interpreted as writing a financial bond, while writing a financial bond is interpreted as cupping.

Changing homes is interpreted as travel, while travel is interpreted as changing homes.

Drought in a dream is better than irrigation. Poverty in a dream is better than wealth. Seeing oneself in a dream being struck, injured and slandered is better than seeing oneself in a dream as the one who strikes, the one who causes injury and the slanderer.

---

[1] Sūrah an-Nūr 24:55

Dream Interpretation Changing Due to an Addition or Subtraction

The interpretation of the dream could change if something is added or subtracted. For example, seeing oneself crying in a dream is happiness; but if the sound of wailing is added then it is a calamity. Laughing in a dream is sadness but if smiling accompanies it, then it is joy.

Nut: A nut in a dream represents hidden treasure, but if you hear the nut cracking then it is a dispute.

Oil: Oil on the head is beautification. If it runs down the face it is sorrow and grief.

Saffron: Saffron is good praise; but if there appears weight or volume to it, then it is sickness.

A sick person: A sick person who leaves his home and does not speak, then this signifies his death. If he speaks, it signifies he will be cured.

Mouse: A mouse represents women if the mouse is only one color. If the mouse has various colors, black and white, then this represents the day and the night.

Fish: Fish represent women if the number of fish is known. If the number is not known it represents spoils of war.

Dream Interpretation According to the Condition of the Person Dreaming

The interpretation of the dream could change from its origin according to the condition of the person dreaming.

Rancor: Rancor in a dream is hated; but as it relates to a righteous person, it is him refraining his hand from evil.

A man came to ibn Sireen and said: "I saw myself in a dream as though I was calling the *adhān*." Ibn Sireen said to him: "Go perform Hajj." Another man came to him with the same dream. Ibn Sireen interpreted his dream as his hand would be cut off due to theft. When Ibn Sireen was asked about the two different interpretations for the same dream, he said: "I saw good conduct from the first man, so I interpreted his dream based upon the statement of Allāh ﷻ:

﴿ وَأَذِّن فِي النَّاسِ بِالْحَجِّ ﴿٢٧﴾ ﴾

And proclaim to mankind the Hajj.[1]

I did not see the same from the second man, thus I interpreted his dream based on the statement of Allāh ﷻ:

﴿ ثُمَّ أَذَّنَ مُؤَذِّنٌ أَيَّتُهَا الْعِيرُ إِنَّكُمْ لَسَارِقُونَ ﴿٧٠﴾ ﴾

Then an announcer called out, 'O caravan, indeed you are thieves.[2]'"

[1] Sūrah al-Ḥaj 22:27
[2] Sūrah Yūsūf 12:70

The person may see in his dream exactly what will occur in his life; be it Hajj, the return of someone absent, something good, or a disaster. The Prophet ﷺ was shown the conquest of Mecca in his dream, and it occurred just as he saw it. Allāh, the Blessed and Exalted, said:

﴿ لَّقَدْ صَدَقَ اللَّهُ رَسُولَهُ الرُّؤْيَا بِالْحَقِّ ﴾ ٢٧

Certainly has Allāh shown to His Messenger the vision in truth.[1]

The person may see something occur to a person in his dream; but the interpretation is for the son or relative of that person, or someone with the same name. The Prophet ﷺ saw a dream in which 'Abū Jahl gave him the pledge of allegiance. But this occurred with 'Ikramah, the son of 'Abū Jahl, when 'Ikramah embraced Islām. When this occurred, the Prophet ﷺ said: "This is it." Meaning this is the interpretation of my dream.

'Asīd ibn 'Abī al-'Īṣ was seen in a dream as governor of Mecca, but this occurred for his son 'Attāb ibn 'Asīd. The Prophet ﷺ appointed him as governor of Mecca.[2]

[1] Sūrah al-Fatḥ 48:27
[2] *Explanation of the Sunnah* by al-Baghawī 12/220-225

CHAPTER *Three*

Dream Interpretation Explained by Ibn al-Qayyim

The basis for interpreting dreams—which are a part of prophecy and revelation—is based upon deductive reasoning and examples that are understood by perception and the intellect.

Shirt: Do you not see that a shirt is interpreted as the religion? Therefore, the shirts seen in a dream may be long or short, clean or filthy. The Prophet ﷺ interpreted a shirt as religion and knowledge. The correlation between the shirt, and religion and knowledge, is that both of them conceal the person and beautify him in front of the people.

Milk: Milk is interpreted as the natural disposition because both of them provide the necessary nourishment for life and a complete upbringing. If the person is left alone, and he is not turned away from milk, then he will grow up preferring it to everything else. Likewise, is the natural disposition of Islām, what Allāh ﷻ created the people upon.

Cow: The cow is interpreted as the people of religion and goodness, those who cultivate the earth. This is the example of the cow. It cultivates the lands without its evil; it brings a lot of good and fulfills the needs of the land and the people. For this reason, when the Prophet ﷺ saw in a dream that cows were slaughtered, he interpreted the cows as his companions.

Farming: Farming and tiling the land are interpreted as action, because the worker either sows good or evil. It is a must that what he seeded comes out, just as the seeds of the farmer come out of the earth. This world is the farm, the actions are the seeds, and the Day of Judgment is when the harvest will produce; and each person will reap their harvest.

Propped wood: Propped wood is interpreted as the hypocrites. The similarity between the two is the hypocrite doesn't have within him a soul or fruits. Thus, his status is that of a piece of wood. For this reason, Allāh ﷻ compared the hypocrites to propped up wood because they are bodies void of faith and goodness. The reason for the similitude to wood that is propped up is because in order for wood to bring about benefit it will be placed in the ceiling or the wall, or any place where it is presumed to benefit. But if it is placed off to the side it does not bring about any benefit; it is only one piece of wood holding up another piece of wood. Thus, He ﷻ compared the hypocrites to wood which is propped up because they don't bring about any benefit.

Fire: Fire is interpreted as *fitnah* (trials and tribulations) due to the harm caused by them to everything they pass by or touch. Fire burns furniture, possessions and bodies; while *fitnah* burns the hearts, the religion and faith.

Stars: Stars are interpreted as the scholars because both of them provide guidance for the inhabitants of the earth. The elevation of the scholars among the people is like the elevation of the stars.

Rain: Rain is interpreted as mercy, knowledge, the Qur'ān, wisdom, and rectification for the people.

Blood: The loss of blood is interpreted as the loss of wealth because both are needed to maintain the body.

Accidents: Accidents seen in a dream relate to the religion. Thus, minor accidents are minor sins, while major accidents are major sins.

Jews and Christians: Jews and Christians are interpreted as innovation in the religion. The Jew represents corrupt intention and following other than the truth. The Christian represents corrupt knowledge, ignorance and misguidance.

Iron: Iron and various weapons represent strength and victory according to the status of the weapon.

Odors: A pleasant fragrance represents good praise, good speech and good actions, while a foul smell represents the opposite.

Scale: A scale represents justice.

Locusts: Locusts represent an army that converges upon the people.

Bees: Bees represent those who consume that which is lawful and wholesome, and they perform righteous actions.

Rooster: A rooster represents a highly respected, celebrated man.

Snake: A snake represents an enemy or a person of innovation that destroys with his poison.

Insects: Insects represent the despicable scoundrels from men.

Mole: A mole represents a blind man who begs from the people.

Wolf: A wolf represents a cheating, oppressive, treacherous, wicked man.

Fox: A fox represents a deceitful, cunning man who is devious toward the truth.

Dog: A dog represents a weak enemy that makes a lot of noise, and his evil is within his speech and his slander. Or an innovator who follows his desires such that it harms his religion.

Cat: A cat represents a slave or servant that goes around to the inhabitants of the home.

Mouse: A mouse represents a wicked, sinful woman.

Lion: A lion represent a dominating man.

Ram: A ram represent an invincible man who is followed.

Every container for water is indicative of furnishings; while every container for wealth, such as a box or a bag, is indicative of the heart. Everything that mixes and blends together is indicative of a partnership, cooperation or marriage. Everything that falls down from an elevated place is blameworthy. Everything that elevates to a lofty place is praiseworthy if it does not exceed the normal height befitting to it. Everything that is burned by fire, then it is a tragedy; and its rectification and life is not expected. Everything that is lost or stolen when the thief is not seen, then its return is not expected. As for those things that are stolen in a dream but the thief is seen, then it is hoped it shall be returned. Every article of clothing that is seen in the wrong place, then this is hated; such as the turban upon the feet, the sock on the head, or the necklace upon the shin.

If the person sees himself with feathers or wings, he will come into wealth; if he flies, he will travel. If the sick person exits his home in silence, this is indicative of his death. If he speaks, this is indicative of his life.

Exiting from a tight doorway is indicative of safety from evil. The tightness is indicative of his repentance, especially if he exits to a wide space; then this is pure good. Travelling from one place to another indicates a change in situation according to the places. Whoever while sleeping returns to the place he was while awake, returns to what he left off from good or evil.

Dying: The dying of a person in a dream can represent his repentance and returning to Allāh. Allāh ﷻ said:

﴿ ثُمَّ رُدُّوا إِلَى اللَّهِ مَوْلَاهُمُ الْحَقِّ ﴿٦٢﴾ ﴾

Then they are returned to Allāh, their True Master.[1]

---

[1] Sūrah al-'An'ām 6:62

A dream of something pawned indicates a debt toward a right of Allāh ﷻ or a right due toward His slaves. A sick person bidding farewell to his family indicates his death.

In summary, all of what was mentioned from the examples from the Qur'ān, and other than that, is from the principles of dream interpretation for those who are skilled in doing so by utilizing the evidence. Likewise, those that understand the Qur'ān are able to interpret dreams in the best manner. The basis of correct interpretation is taken from the lamp of the Qur'ān. Thus, a ship is interpreted as safety due to the statement of Allāh ﷻ.

﴿ فَأَنجَيْنَاهُ وَأَصْحَابَ السَّفِينَةِ ﴿١٥﴾ ﴾

Then We saved him and those with him in the ship.[1]

Trade and wood are interpreted as the hypocrites. Stones are interpreted as the hardness of the heart. Eggs are interpreted as women, as are clothes. Drinking water is interpreted as *fitnah*. Eating flesh is interpreted as backbiting.

Keys are interpreted as earnings, treasure and wealth. Opening a door is sometimes interpreted as *du'ā'*, and sometimes as victory. Seeing a place in which one cannot enter indicates humiliation and corruption upon its people. A rope indicates a covenant, the truth and support.

Sleepiness: Sleepiness can be interpreted as safety.

Onions: For the person that takes them in a dream, onions, legumes, garlic, and lentils indicate he will take something lowly in exchange for

[1] Sūrah al-'Ankabūt 29:15

something better from wealth, provision, knowledge, a spouse, or a home.

Sickness: Sickness is interpreted as hypocrisy, doubt, and the desire of showing off.

Nursing child: A nursing child is interpreted as the enemy. This is based on the statement of Allāh ﷻ:

﴿ فَالْتَقَطَهُ آلُ فِرْعَوْنَ لِيَكُونَ لَهُمْ عَدُوًّا وَحَزَنًا ﴿٨﴾ ﴾

Then the household of Pharaoh picked him up, that he might become for them an enemy and a cause of grief.[1]

Sand: Sand is interpreted as an invalid action. This is based upon the statement of the Exalted:

﴿ مَّثَلُ الَّذِينَ كَفَرُوا بِرَبِّهِمْ ۖ أَعْمَالُهُمْ كَرَمَادٍ اشْتَدَّتْ بِهِ الرِّيحُ فِي يَوْمٍ عَاصِفٍ ﴿١٨﴾ ﴾

The parable of those who disbelieve in their Lord is that their works are as ashes, on which the wind blows furiously on a stormy day.[2]

Marriage represents building and construction, light represents guidance, and darkness represents misguidance.

---

[1] Sūrah al-Qaṣaṣ 28:8
[2] Sūrah 'Ibrāhīm 14:18

Dream Interpretation of the Pious Predecessors

'Umār ibn al-Khaṭṭāb ﷺ appointed a man named Hābis ibn Sa'd al-Ṭā'y as a judge. Hābis said to 'Umār: "O leader of the believers, I had a dream in which I saw the sun and the moon fighting, while the stars were evenly divided amongst them." 'Umār said: "Which side were you fighting on?" Hābis said: "I was with the moon against the sun." 'Umār said: "You were with the vanishing sign. Go away. You cannot work for me. You will only fight during a confused situation." Hābis later fought in the Battle of Ṣiffīn[1] alongside Mu'āwiyah, and he was killed in the battle.

It was said to a person who interprets dreams: "I saw the sun and moon inside of me." He said to him: "You are going to die." He used as evidence the statement of Allāh ﷻ:

﴿ فَإِذَا بَرِقَ الْبَصَرُ ﴿٧﴾ وَخَسَفَ الْقَمَرُ ﴿٨﴾ وَجُمِعَ الشَّمْسُ وَالْقَمَرُ ﴿٩﴾
يَقُولُ الْإِنسَانُ يَوْمَئِذٍ أَيْنَ الْمَفَرُّ ﴿١٠﴾ ﴾

So, when the sight shall be dazed, and the moon will be eclipsed, and the sun and the moon are joined, on that Day man will say: "Where (is the refuge) to flee?"[2]

---

[1] Translator's note: The Battle of Ṣiffīn was the battle between the two Muslims armies, one lead by 'Alī ibn 'Abī Ṭālib, the other lead by Mu'awiyah.

[2] Sūrah al-Qiyāmah 75:7-10

A man said to Ibn Sireen: “I saw with me in a dream four loaves of bread and the sunset.” Ibn Sireen said to him: “You will die in four days.” Then he recited the statement of the Exalted:

﴿ ثُمَّ جَعَلْنَا الشَّمْسَ عَلَيْهِ دَلِيلًا ﴿٤٥﴾ ثُمَّ قَبَضْنَاهُ إِلَيْنَا قَبْضًا يَسِيرًا ﴿٤٦﴾ ﴾

Then We made the sun for it an indication. Then We withdraw it to Us a gradual concealed withdrawal.[1]

Based on this interpretation, he had four days’ worth of provisions before he would die.

Another man said to him: “I saw in a dream a bag filled with dirt.” Ibn Sireen said to him: “You are going to die.” Then he recited the verse:

﴿ فَلَمَّا قَضَيْنَا عَلَيْهِ الْمَوْتَ مَا دَلَّهُمْ عَلَىٰ مَوْتِهِ إِلَّا دَابَّةُ الْأَرْضِ ﴿١٤﴾ ﴾

Then when We decreed death for him (Sulaymān), nothing informed them (jinn) of his death, except a little worm of the earth.[2]

Date tree: The date tree indicates a Muslim man upon the good word, while the colocynth indicates the opposite.

Idol: An idol represents an evil person who brings no benefit.

Garden: A garden represents actions. The burning of a garden represents the invalidity of the action. This is based upon the example found in the Qur’ān.

---

[1] Sūrah al-Furqān 25:45-46
[2] Sūrah Saba' 34:14

Yarn: Whoever sees his yard being untied or his garment falling apart, then his servant will break his contract with him.

Walking: If someone sees himself in a dream walking upright on a straight path, this indicates he is upright upon the straight path. The person who sees himself taking a narrow path, this indicates him turning away from it for what opposes it. If he sees two paths—one on the right and one on the left—and he takes one of the paths, then he is from those people.

Uncovering: A person's private area becoming uncovered in a dream indicates a sin he commits and is exposed for.

Fleeing and running from something indicates success. Drowning in water represents a tribulation in his worldly affairs and his religion. If he sees a rope suspended between the heavens and the earth, and he holds onto it, this is his holding onto the Book of Allāh ﷻ and adhering to His rope. If it breaks, then he loses his protection unless he entrusted the rope to someone else in his dream. As this may indicate he will be killed, or he will die.[1]

[1] *I'lām al-Muwaq'īn an Rabil 'Alamīn* 1/190-195